NAVIGATING THE UNKNOWN
A Parent's Guide To Supporting A Gay Child

MEL RICHIE

Table of contents

Chapter 1.

Is Your Child Gay?

If your son likes sissy things or your daughter avoids wearing feminine clothing, it is more probable that he or she will deviate from the standard of heterosexuality. The prediction of sexual choice, on the other hand, is still an imprecise science.

An abnormally light, delicate, and effeminate air in a small boy's stride, a fascination with dolls, cosmetics, princesses, and gowns, and a strong disdain for physical play with other boys are all cliches that we are all familiar with. The overly manly attitude, possibly a predilection for tools, a square-jawed eagerness for physical tussles with males, and an antipathy to all the scented and delicate trappings of femininity are all characteristics that are found in young girls.

In addition to being feared and disliked, these patterns of conduct are often discussed directly as indicators of adult homosexuality.

Nevertheless, developmental scientists have only just begun to undertake controlled research to uncover the earliest and most reliable markers of adult homosexuality. These studies have only been done relatively recently.

In the process of meticulously examining the childhoods of gay people, researchers are discovering a fascinating set of behavioral indications that gays seem to have in common. Strangely enough, the homophobic anxieties that have been around for a long time and are held by many parents have some true predictive currency.

Both J. Michael Bailey and Kenneth J. Zucker, who are both psychologists, contributed to the publication of a significant work on the subject of homosexuality in children in the year 1995. Both Bailey and Zucker investigated sex-typed behavior, which is a lengthy list of intrinsic sex differences in the actions of young men and young girls. This list is now considered to be the standard in the scientific community.

In many research, experts have established that these sex differences are virtually immune to learning. They are also seen in every culture surveyed. Of course, there are exceptions to the norm; it is only when examining the aggregate data that sex differences soar into the stratosphere of statistical significance.

The most prominent distinctions are in the sphere of play. Boys participate in what developmental psychologists refer to as "rough-and-tumble play." Girls prefer the companionship of toys over a knee in the ribs.

Toy interests are another important sex difference, with males gravitating toward toy machine guns and monster trucks and girls orienting toward baby dolls and highly gendered figurines. Young children of both sexes enjoy pretend play, but the roles inside the fantasy framework are gender-segregated by age two.

Girls perform the role of, for instance, cooing moms, ballerinas, or fairy princesses, whereas males like to be warriors and superheroes. Not unexpectedly, then, males instinctively prefer other guys for playmates, whereas girls would much rather play with other girls.

So based on some earlier, shakier research, along with a good dose of common sense, Bailey and Zucker hypothesized that homosexuals would show an inverted pattern of sex-typed childhood behaviors—little boys preferring girls as playmates and becoming infatuated with their mother's makeup kit; little girls strangely enamored of field hockey or professional wrestling—that sort of thing.

Empirically, the authors say, there are two approaches to examining this theory, using either prospective or retrospective research. Using the prospective technique, young children demonstrating sex-atypical tendencies are tracked throughout adolescence and early adulthood so that their sexual orientation may be determined at maturity.

This strategy is not tremendously practical for various reasons. Given that a tiny fraction of the population is gay, prospective studies need a high number of offspring. This technique likewise takes a long period, roughly 16 years. Finally, not a lot of parents are going to offer their children. Right or wrong, this is a delicate issue, and normally it is only children who display major sex-atypical behaviors that are brought into clinics and whose cases are made accessible to researchers.

Rough-and-Tumble Girls

For example, in 2008 research psychologist Kelley Drummond and her colleagues interviewed 25 adult women who were sent by their parents for examination at a mental health clinic when they were between three and 12 years old. At the time, all these females exhibited multiple diagnostic symptoms of gender identity disorder. They could have strongly chosen male playmates, insisted on wearing guys' attire, enjoyed the rough-and-tumble play, said that they would soon develop a penis, or refused to pee in a sitting posture. Although only 12 percent of these women grew up to have gender dysphoria (the uncomfortable sense that your biological sex does not match your gender), the odds of these women reporting a bisexual or homosexual orientation were up to 23 times higher than would occur in a general sample of young women. Not all tomboys become lesbians, of course, but these statistics imply that lesbians commonly have a history of cross-sex-typed activities.

And the same applies to homosexual males. Bailey and Zucker, who performed retrospective research in which participants answered questions about their history, reported that 89 percent of randomly chosen homosexual males remembered cross-sex-typed childhood behaviors above the heterosexual median.

Critics have stated that individuals' recollections may be modified to align with society's expectations and prejudices. But in a brilliant research published in 2008 in Developmental Psychology, data from childhood home films corroborated this retrospective strategy. People blindly coded kid targets on the latter's sex-typical behaviors, as exhibited on the screen. The scientists discovered that "those targets who, as adults, identified themselves as homosexual were judged to be gender nonconforming as children."

Numerous studies have now repeated this general trend, indicating a robust relationship between childhood departures from gender role standards and adult sexual orientation. There is also evidence of a "dosage effect": the more gender-nonconforming features there are in infancy, the more probable it is that a gay or bisexual orientation would be present in adulthood.

Not all young boys who enjoy wearing dresses grow up to be homosexual, nor do all little girls who dislike skirts become lesbians. Many will be straight, and others, let's not forget, will be transsexuals.

I was quite androgynous, demonstrating a mosaic pattern of sex-typical and abnormal behaviors. Despite my parents' favorite idea that I was merely a young Casanova, Zucker, and Bailey's results may explain that old Polaroid photo in which 11 of the 13 other children at my seventh birthday party are small ladies. But I wasn't an overtly effeminate youngster, was never teased as a "sissy" and, by the time I was 10, was indistinguishably as obnoxious, boorish, and wired as my close male contemporaries.

On the Monkey Bars

In fact, by age 13, I was severely indoctrinated into male standards. I took up middle school wrestling as a very thin 80-pound eighth grader, and in so doing, unfortunately, became all too cognizant of my gay inclination.

Cross-cultural studies reveal that prehomosexual males are more drawn to solitary activities such as swimming, cycling, and tennis than they are to rougher contact sports like football and soccer; they are also less likely to be childhood bullies. In any case, I remember being with the ladies on the monkey bars at recess in second grade while the males were on the field playing football and looking over at them, thinking to myself how it was unusual. I pondered why anybody would want to behave that way.

Researchers easily accept that there are very likely multiple—and no doubt exceedingly complicated—developmental paths to adult homosexuality. Heritable, biological elements combine with contextual events to determine sexual orientation. Because the data often reveal very early emerging traits in homosexuals, children who show pronounced sex-atypical behaviors may have more of a genetic loading to their homosexuality, whereas gay adults who were sex-typical as children might trace their homosexuality more directly to particular childhood experiences.

Then we come to the most essential issue of all. Why do parents worry so much about whether their kid may or may not be gay? All else being equal, I suppose we would be hard-pressed to find parents who would truly desire their kids to be gay. Evolutionarily, parental homophobia is a no-brainer: homosexual sons and lesbian daughters are not likely to breed (unless they get inventive).

But take this in mind, parents, there are more ways for your kid to contribute to your overall genetic progress than monotonous sexual reproduction. I don't know how much money or residual fame is trickling down to, say, k. d. lang, Elton John, and Rachel Maddow's close relatives, but I can only imagine that these straight kin are far better off in terms of their reproductive opportunities than they would be without a homosexual dangling so magnificently on their family trees.

So develop your tiny homosexual inherent skills, and your final genetic payback may, curiously enough, be even bigger with one extremely remarkable gay kid than it would be if 10 average straight children burst from your loins.

If researchers ultimately master the predicting of adult sexual orientation in youngsters, will parents want to know? I can say as a previously prehomosexual pipsqueak that any preparation on the side of others would have made it simpler on me, rather than continually dreading rejection or worrying about some accidental slipup leading to my "exposure." It would have at least prevented all those uncomfortable, continuous inquiries throughout my teenage years about why I wasn't dating a lovely attractive girl (or questions from the nice pretty girl about why I was dating her and refusing her advances).

And another thing: it must be quite hard to stare into your homosexual toddler's limpid eyes, wipe away the cookie crumbs from her face, and put her out on the streets for being gay.

Chapter 2.

Coming Out: Information for Parents of LGBTQ Child

"Coming out" is a lifetime process of knowing, admitting, and revealing one's gender identity and/or sexual orientation with others. It may be fast and simple for some, or longer and more challenging for others.

Parents of lesbian, gay, bisexual, transgender, and questioning (LGBTQ) youth must realize each kid is unique and will have their own experiences and emotions along the road.

"I feel different from other kids..."
sensations of being "different" occur throughout childhood, but it may not be evident to the kid what the sensations imply. Children may begin exploring gender and relationships before kindergarten, so "coming out" and expressing these experiences of being different from others may happen at any time.

For many youngsters, gender identity becomes obvious during puberty when they acquire gender features and greater love attachments. However, many LGBTQ kids have reported, in hindsight, that they started to detect something "different" about themselves early in childhood, particularly for gender-varied youth, sometimes as far back as preschool. See Gender Diverse & Transgender Children.

It is typical for LGBTQ kids to feel terrified or apprehensive in this era. Some might start to feel alienated from their classmates, particularly if they feel that they don't fit in or are given a hard time for being different. Just remember that children who feel loved and accepted for who they are have a lot easier time.

Parents and families may: Play a crucial role in advocating for safe locations where their kids can explore hobbies without judgment or prejudices.

Support various friendships and social activities without concentrating on expectations surrounding gender.

Provide exposure to persons working and enjoying activities outside of typical gender standards.

Engage in talks and check periodically with your children about their hobbies, friend groups, romantic inclinations, and any bullying or taunting that may be going place.

"I think I might be gay (or lesbian, bi, or trans), but I'm not sure, and I don't know how I feel about that..."

Beyond merely feeling "different," young individuals begin to question whether they could be "gay" (or lesbian, bi, or trans) or any other term they may want. Many kids have conflicting sentiments when they first try on a new way of identifying. It might be a combination of exhilaration, relief, and fear.

Many youngsters may strive to hide these sensations to suit social standards, to fit in, or even to avoid offending their parents or relatives. In other situations, kids could be overwhelmed by all these sensations, which raises the risk of depression, anxiety, and other mental health concerns. For example, people may distance themselves from others for fear of being revealed or "outed."

Some kids may feel quite alone, particularly if they reside in a place that doesn't have an active LGBTQ-youth support system.

Having a friendly and helpful atmosphere at home and excellent connections with peers can allow kids to control their emotions and cope with any prejudice they may experience.

"I accept that I'm gay, but what will my family and friends say?"
Teens may understand that they are LGBTQ but are not quite ready to start sharing this fact with anybody yet. Some may feel comfortable being upfront about their identity, while other teenagers may not tell anybody for a long time. Teens may hunt for signals on how they feel about their gender identity and sexual orientation. Speaking favorably about LGBTQ personalities or current events you will let them know you are supportive of their identity.

Society has been more open and tolerant of LGBTQ persons, and young people are starting to come out at younger ages than they did a decade ago. Children may initially come out to online networks or classmates they see as safe and welcoming before notifying their families.

Parents and children must recognize that acceptance is a process that encompasses the whole family. Just as it takes time and support for LGBTQ children to understand and embrace their identity, this is also true for parents.
"I've told most of my family and friends that I'm gay (or lesbian, bi, or trans)."
Teens feel safe enough in who they are and share that knowledge with loved ones. It takes bravery and fortitude for a young person to disclose who they are, particularly for kids who are afraid of how their family would react. They may be terrified of failing or angering their family, or in certain situations may dread being physically attacked or expelled from their homes.

Again, parents frequently require time to react to the news. It may take them days, weeks, or even months to come to grips with their child's sexuality or gender identity. But parents must express love and support for their kids, even if they don't entirely grasp everything.

Coming out to others may be a freeing experience, particularly for those youth who are supported by their communities and families. LGBTQ youth may feel comfortable talking freely about their thoughts and maybe love relationships for the first time. For transgender and gender-diverse youth, they may now feel free to begin expressing themselves authentically as the gender they feel within.

Parents and families can: When your kid shares their identity with you, react in an affirming, supportive manner. Understand that while gender identity is not possible to be altered, it typically is revealed over time as individuals learn more about themselves.

Accept and adore your kids as they are. Try to comprehend what they are feeling and experiencing. Even if there are arguments, kids will need your support and affirmation to grow into healthy teenagers and adults.

Stand up for your kids when they are mistreated. Do not dismiss the social pressure or bullying your kid may be undergoing. See How You Can Help Your Child Avoid & Address Bullying.

Make it clear that insults or jokes based on gender, gender identity, or sexual orientation are not acceptable. Express your dislike of these sorts of jokes or slurs when you see them in the community or media.

Be on the watch for danger indicators that may suggest a need for mental health help such as anxiety, insecurity, sadness, poor self-esteem, and other emotional disorders in your kid and others who may not have a source of support otherwise.

Connect your kid with LGBTQ groups, services, and events. They must know they are not alone.

Celebrate diversity in all forms. Provide access to a range of books, videos, and materials—including those that favorably reflect gender-diverse persons. Point out LGBTQ celebrities and role models who speak up for the LGBTQ community, and individuals in general who display courage in the face of societal censure.

Support your child's self-expression. Engage in talks with them concerning their choices of dress, jewelry, haircut, friends, and room décor.

Reach out for information, resources, and assistance if you feel the need to enhance your awareness of LGBTQ adolescent experiences. See Support Resources for Families of Gender Diverse Youth.

Remember

Even if you are having problems comprehending your kid's identity or emotions, not retreating from your position as a parent is probably one of the most crucial ways to assist a child continue to experience a sense of being cared for and welcomed.

Feeling loved is crucial to the overall health and development of all children regardless of gender or sexual orientation. Many parents require their assistance to help them understand and manage their challenging feelings and worries during a child's "coming out."

The process of announcing a gay identity is commonly dubbed 'coming out'. It may start:

With gay fantasies or dreams; When a person discovers she is attracted to someone of the same gender; With a sensation that she is different from her peers and classmates; or With a sexual encounter.

These sentiments may generate confusion for a young person and might be made worse by:

the societal stigma that may come with homosexuality; a lack of knowledge; a dearth of LGBT role models; or few chances to connect with other youths who are experiencing similar sentiments.

It may be extremely tough for kids to decide to inform their parents about their gay identity. They may despise the concept that they are 'lying' by not informing their parents, but they also worry about how their parents would respond.

Sometimes parents think that their adolescent is homosexual. However, sometimes what you consider to be true is not. Wait until your adolescent is ready to discuss. Some teenagers are not ready to reveal their sexuality until they are adults. If there is a gay theme in a comic strip or on a TV program, you may talk about it, hopefully finding a way to let your son or daughter know that they are loved no matter what their orientation.

Some teenagers may tell a sibling or relative before they tell a parent, and typically they will pick one parent to inform first.

Parents occasionally bring their adolescent to the doctor for a 'diagnosis'. They can't believe what their adolescent is telling them. There is no blood test or other definite technique of knowing whether someone is homosexual.

Chapter 3.

How to react to your child coming out as gay

Every coming-out is distinctive and there is no right or wrong way to do it. But, if your kid comes out to you, there are things you can do to make it easier for you both

Much of parenting is instinctual — from dad jokes, being a personal chauffeur, or a personal finance manager, to the important issues like punishment and being a shoulder to cry on. But it's true what they say: there's no handbook. Society is developing, young people feel more empowered to express their sexuality and/or gender; progress isn't waiting for us to catch up. As open-minded as you are, you may still find yourself startled if your kid comes out to you. Never fear: we're here to help you manage it like a pro.

Let them lead the way
You may have had your suspicions. Coming out is a watershed moment, a great discharge of anxiety, hope, relief, excitement, and rage - a lot is going on. If you sense they're on the brink, tell them you've noticed there's something on their mind, that they can trust you if anything is upsetting them. Gentle nudges, sure; assertions and announcements – "You're trans, aren't you?" – maybe not. The words should come from them: this is their movie and we're simply extras.

quiet, quiet, calm, calm
Coming out isn't necessarily a sugary, Hollywood moment. Sometimes it occurs during conflicts, in wrath, the words yelled at you. Stay Zen. Listen. Nod to demonstrate

you're listening. Wait until you estimate they're done and then, rather than giving them your opinion or turning it back to you, give them power and ask if they want to hear what you think.

Be ready
Frustrating as it could be, they may not be ready to chat right immediately. Chances are the coming out didn't go like they'd planned or intended — they may be in shock that it's out there. Going from "in" to "out" is a tremendous shift of status. Offer your support and an ear when they need it, whenever that happens to be. That time will surely arrive.

Instant responses
You don't have to sit there and say nada, however. You're human, after all. Good responses include:

"I'm so glad you told me." However you feel about the news, your kid has trusted you with something that's resided inside of them forever. LGBTQ+ youth don't simply tell everyone at first. You should feel honored; tell them you are. Ask them how they're feeling now they've informed you; it gives them time to digest.

Hug. Kids will be kids and could turn their nose up at physical touch – but put it on the table and watch what happens.

"Have you told anybody else?" Don't be upset, but it's doubtful you're the first they've told. Often an LGBTQ+ youngster may tell friends and may try another adult – possibly someone close to you – to use as a sounding board. Your youngster realizes there's less baggage between them and someone they don't know as well as you. This question should comfort you — at least they haven't been going through this alone. An LGBTQ+ person spends their whole life coming out to someone and... it doesn't always go well. But you may aspire to be different. Talking to your youngster about how the other disclosures went might be a nice diversion until they're ready to discuss more about how they're feeling. It benefits you too: if they've previously confided in someone else you know, you can speak to this person without breaking either confidence.

"Do you need me to do anything or talk to anyone?" Coming out isn't always an issue they need addressing, generally they want a nice ear, but it's typically very taxing, and... they may need you to inform Grandma. Best not to urge your kid to avoid telling anybody - honestly, your senior relatives will cope – since it signals it's something shameful, but you may coach them on anticipated responses and advise prudence if need be. If they vow confidentiality, respect that request to your death.

Maybe don't say:

"I already knew!" Some LGBTQ+ persons tell me it may be reassuring knowing close friends and family were already aware - it makes it seem like less of a major issue. Others are terrified that they either didn't conceal their secret very well or that everyone was chatting behind their back.

To be on the safe side, don't declare you already know until they ask you - although the sparkling confetti and inflatable unicorns dropping from the ceiling may give it away. Be honest, but polite, and focus on emotional indicators rather than remarking on, for example, their childhood habits or a propensity to favor toys or outfits not generally associated with their gender. Try: "You're my child and I've watched you grow up.

Yes, I knew there was something wonderful inside you that one day you'd tell me about." It seems schmaltzy but, when started from the heart, it makes all the difference and may establish a link between you. That's not to say you can't laugh about it, because comedy helps as an opener, but read the room, and follow their lead. We LGBTQ+ crew take this very seriously, probably overly so at times, yeah, but this is our thing.

"It's just a phase!" Stop. Let's not think heterosexuality or being cisgender is the "default" that we must aim for, or that with a little encouragement, your kid will fall "back" in line. Any youngster coming out to you is alerting you this is who they are; this is their default setting.

"It's such a waste." I believe when parents say this they mean the life they had plotted out for their kid will never be. But you cannot, and should not, grieve a person who never was or regrets a fate that wasn't yours to choose. Instead, focus on the kid the universe has given you. Not growing up heterosexual or cisgender shouldn't prohibit them from accomplishing most things they want to do. The true waste would've been your kid living a falsehood.

"I read somewhere..." There's been a flood of unpleasant and deceptive news about the LGBTQ+ community in recent years – notably trans and nonbinary persons. Best not to regurgitate this back at your youngster - chances are they've read it too if they know your login information for newspaper paywalls. Allow the lived experience of LGBTQ+ individuals to be your guide, if you want, but you should allow your child's ideas and emotions to dictate your response and your support. You may not "agree" with this circumstance yet your approval is not necessary.

Your love and strength are essential, however. The world is challenging and this certainly bothers you - do you want to make it worse? Toothpaste virtually ever goes back in the tube without producing an appalling mess; you're unlikely to persuade them they should choose a different route and you should surely not die trying.

Read the label
Forget jokes about pronouns, wokeness, identity politics, or dismal stereotypes. Yes, labels are now more diversified from what you knew growing up. Your youngster could be pleased to identify as homosexual or may just choose to identify as someone questioning their sexuality. Labels are helpful for us: they help us tell the world who we are. But we get to pick them and we may also opt not to utilize them. It simply takes a second or two more to think about it. You'll get it wrong, at first maybe. Just listen with an open mind, show an interest, and attempt to do better. Ask questions if you don't understand, but if your kid can't precisely articulate what it means to them directly, it doesn't make their experience any less real. And, sure, ask which pronouns

they prefer: she/her, he/him, or they. It takes an additional few seconds to think about; make the time.

Getting personal

There's more to being LGBTQ+ than sex and queries about your child's sex life will still go down like a cup of cold sickness whatever their orientation. Mind your own business on this, just remind them to be careful. If your kid is trans, you'll be wondering about what this means for their future. It doesn't always indicate they'll desire or require medical assistance of any type - seek instruction from them before you race in with inquiries. They may not have the solutions, but they still know who they are. Respect that.

Warriors vs champions

It's a sad reality that LGBTQ+ persons have a rougher time. Your first inclination as a parent is to safeguard your offspring. You'll want to crush skulls, mend bullies, warn off prospective love rats, and blow out at racists. This is your kid; you want to be a fighter for them. Trouble is... it's probably the last thing they want. They won't desire protecting, or defending, or for you to give out ceremonial beatings. They may end up resenting you for intervening.

Instead, be a champion. Fight your kid's corner by invitation, by encouragement. There's no way you'll be able to take all the trash coming an LGBTQ+ person's way. Human nature never disappoints. If your youngster is young or afraid about what being LGBTQ+ implies for their future, comfort them.

Tell them you know some people don't understand or accept their differences, but bigots never win. You'll always be there to listen, assist and understand. Remind them this is a fresh beginning, that the world can be theirs, and that you're proud of them. But let them find their path — this is one automobile you can't drive.

Being calm, open-minded, and supportive of your LGBTQ+ kid is the closest you'll come to being a superhero. Use your abilities for good, wear your cape with pride – and fly.

Chapter 4.

Responding in Love to an Adult Gay Child

As a parent, it can be challenging to navigate your relationship with an adult gay child. There are certain things that you can do to ensure that your child feels loved, accepted, and supported. Firstly, it's important to approach the situation with an open mind and heart. Acknowledge your child's sexuality and make it clear that your love for them is unconditional. This means that you will always be there for them, no matter what.

Listening to your child's experiences and feelings without judgment is crucial in building a strong and trusting relationship. Your child needs to know that they can come to you with anything and that you will always be there to support them. Try to understand their perspective and show empathy towards their experiences.

Remember that your child's sexuality is just one aspect of who they are, and it doesn't define them entirely. Show them that you are interested in their life beyond their sexuality. Ask them about their hobbies, interests, and career aspirations. This will show them that you see them as a whole person and not just as a gay child.

Creating a positive and accepting environment is key to helping your child thrive. This means being open to their partners and friends and treating them with respect and kindness. By doing so, you can help your child feel loved and accepted for who they are, and not just for their sexuality.

You may feel upset by your child's choice to "come out." But remember, this is not anything they have done "to" you.

If you've ever heard the words "I'm gay" from a son or daughter, the declaration certainly came as the shock of a lifetime. You certainly went through a full inventory of intense emotions: astonishment, bewilderment, wrath, guilt. Then followed the inquiries for you and your spouse: Why did this happen? Where did we fail? And how can we as Christians and loving parents react to our child's avowed homosexuality?

Stephen Arterburn, best-selling author, and renowned Christian psychologist, believes many parents of homosexual children withhold love and compassion because they're frightened to look condoning of the gay lifestyle. The fact is that your youngster needs unconditional love and acceptance more than ever. Withholding affection can only make a tough situation worse. Remember that acceptance is not the same thing as approval. Acceptance involves admitting what is real. It does not imply you must compromise your ideas about what constitutes good and evil, nor does it mean you condone gay conduct and activities.

Chances are your son or daughter fought long and hard with the choice to declare their homosexuality to you. They prepared for judgment and rejection. That's why it's all the more crucial you let them know they are respected and loved as much as ever.

You should feel comfortable sharing your worries about the morality, health hazards, and other dangers linked with the LGBT lifestyle. But don't belabor things. It's extremely crucial that any remarks you make be couched in love. The fundamental message remains: I love you and accept you – that will never change.

You may feel upset by your child's choice to "come out." But remember, this is not anything they have done "to" you. Their homosexuality is not something they dreamt up to purposefully disgrace or harm you. It's most likely been a difficult secret they've kept concealed for years exactly because they thought you would be harmed. This is your child's fight, your child's pain. As a caring parent — and a Christian — you must be mature and bold. Now is the opportunity to teach your kid the same grace and unconditional love that Jesus gives to all of us who battle with sin in our lives. Pray for wisdom, understanding, and the proper things to speak in this tough and sensitive issue.

Withholding affection from your suffering kid can only make a terrible situation worse. You may feel upset by your child's choice to "come out." But remember, this is not anything they have done "to" you.

You may feel a broad array of emotions after finding out your kid is LGBT.

The purpose of your first reaction is to give love and protection while you come up to speed with your kids and where they are. Remember, the finest reply entails a genuine effort to comprehend what they're feeling.

After the talk concludes, you'll likely experience a roller coaster of emotions. Over the following several hours, as you sit with the news, you may discover your response wasn't what you hoped it would have been. Remember, you can never go wrong with a sincere apology.

In circumstances when being homosexual contradicts your values and beliefs, you may feel as if apologizing is comparable to approving their conduct. However, the two are not the same. Therefore, you might give an apology for your emotional response.

Likewise, you may apologize for hurting their sentiments, which doesn't indicate you're approving their decision. For example, you may say, "I'm sorry I hurt your feelings." "I'm sorry about the emotion that was involved."

Remember, there are various ways to give affirmation and an apology without endorsing their actions. For example, ParentGuidance.org provides fantastic tools to aid parents.

As you return to the discussion, own the discomfort if required. It's acceptable to express, "This may be awkward, but I'm genuinely curious." Likewise, you might be truthful and say, "I don't know what to ask or say." Again, emphasizing that your purpose is to comprehend, not to convince or invalidate.

It's alright if you don't know what to do. Now is an excellent moment to lean into

your connection rather than draw away
from it.

Chapter 5.

Tips for Parents of LGBTQ Youth

Parenting isn't always easy - particularly if your kid is lesbian, gay, bisexual, transgender, or questioning (LGBTQ). In many ways no different from their classmates, LGBTQ adolescents encounter some particular issues that parents frequently feel unprepared to manage. To assist, Johns Hopkins pediatric and adolescent medicine expert Errol Fields discusses strategies you can do to keep your kid happy and healthy.

Let them know they are loved
For many LGBTQ adolescents, revealing the news to mom and dad is the toughest aspect

of coming out. "Time and time again, we hear the same thing from patients: 'Once my parents are behind me, I can handle anything else the world throws at me,'" Dr. Fields continues. "You're their anchor, and your acceptance is key. Evidence indicates that LGBTQ teenagers who are accepted by their families grow up to be happier and healthier adults."

You don't need to be an expert in all things LGBTQ to let them know you care. There's no right or wrong way to demonstrate love, say experts: Just be there and be open. Even if you're not sure what to say, something as basic as "I'm here for you. I love you, and I will support you no matter what" can mean the world to your child.

Encourage dialogue
As you're certainly well aware, encouraging your kids to open up sometimes seems difficult. Dr. Fields thinks the best way to achieve this is to create trust and start small.

Be inquisitive about their lives. Get to know their pals and what they enjoy doing. Ask them how their day went and whether they learned anything interesting at school. If it's like pulling teeth at times, don't be disheartened. Children do want to be able to chat with parents about what's going on in their lives.

These talks may seem like no-brainers, but remaining connected to your child's reality makes it simpler for them to approach you with larger, more difficult topics, including sexuality. The more you talk with your kid, the more comfortable they'll feel.

How to Get Them Talking
You can't always depend on your children to begin these discussions, however. When you feel something has to be addressed, consider being less direct. Adolescents frequently have a hard time communicating about themselves. Parents may aid by bringing up their child's friends or personalities you see

when watching age-appropriate movies or television together.

Today's media give plenty of instructional opportunities for parents to grab. While it may appear less personal, it is a chance to tackle tough themes in a manner that's not so intimidating. For instance, if a movie contains a bisexual character, begin a debate by mentioning, "The character in this show is attracted to boys and girls. That's OK with me. What do you think?"

Learn the facts
Parents may have some misunderstandings regarding gender and sexual orientation. Empower your parenting with what professionals know:

It's not "just a phase." Embrace — don't ignore — their emerging sense of self.

There is no "cure." It's not something that has to be corrected.

Don't search for blame. Instead, praise your kids and all that they are.

Stay active with the school
Kids spend nearly as much time in the classroom as they do at home. Here's what you can do to make sure kids feel comfortable there, too.

Advocate for a gay-straight alliance (GSA), which has been proven to make schools safer and enhance academic achievement among LGBTQ students.
Maintain constant communication with instructors. That way, you'll know when troubles develop.
Push for more inclusive sex education. Very few states enable schools to give LGBTQ children the knowledge they need to be safe and healthy. Be aware of these knowledge gaps so that you may fill them yourself.
Above all, don't hesitate to speak out. Parents have a big voice in the educational

system. You do have power. If there's an issue and the school isn't taking your complaints seriously, go to the principal or perhaps the school board.

Look out for symptoms of bullying
Bullying is a concern for all children, but LGBTQ adolescents in particular are routinely targeted for being different. If you spot these indications, speak out to a teacher, guidance counselor, or school administrator:

Behavior change (e.g., your outgoing, social youngster is suddenly withdrawn)
Discipline or behavioral difficulties in school
Declining grades
Unexplained absences
Sudden adjustments in who's a buddy and who's not
Engagement in risk behavior (e.g., drug use, new sexual partner) that is out of character for your kid
Take a team approach

Assisting may be tough at times. It's OK to feel worried, perplexed, or astonished — but don't draw back when you're needed most. At some point, some parents feel so overwhelmed that they simply throw up their hands and declare, "I can't do it." It's a lot for parents to comprehend, but the most essential thing is to prevent leaving their youngsters feeling alone and neglected.

"Remember, your child is having more difficulty with this than you are," adds Dr. Fields, "and your duty as a parent comes first." If you're suffering, call out for assistance. Team up with a physician, a counselor at school, close family members, and even community groups — for example, Parents, Families, and Friends of Lesbians and Gays (PFLAG) — if you're having problems tackling it alone.

Ensure they build good connections
As youngsters reach adolescence, it's OK for them to develop an interest in other boys

and girls their age. "Dating is daunting for most parents — especially parents of LGBTQ youth — but it's an important part of adolescent development for all children," affirms Dr. Fields. To keep children safe, be engaged, and remain connected. "By encouraging your kid to date in a way that's healthy and age-appropriate, you send a powerful message: LGBTQ relationships are normal, and there's nothing to hide or be ashamed of," he adds.

Stay on top of social media
Because they're frequently discouraged from being upfront about their sexual orientation and gender identity, some LGBTQ folks depend on social media and phone apps to meet others. Many social platforms and apps allow LGBTQ adolescents an inclusive environment to communicate with friends and supporters, but others (particularly dating apps) feature information that is unsuitable for minors. Monitor what they're doing on their gadgets and speak to them

about phone and social media usage, suggests Dr. Fields.

"More importantly," adds Dr. Fields, "understand that kids turn to these apps if they feel like they don't have anyone to talk to. Be present so that your kid doesn't need to turn elsewhere for advice and support."

Chapter 6.

What to Do When Your Religious Beliefs Do Not Align With Being Gay

In reaction to your adolescent being homosexual, you may feel the impulse to respond, "We'll pray the gay away." Likewise, you may feel motivated to tell your kid this is a phase or how terrible they are for their decision. However, reactions like these are damaging and even harmful.

You may question, can we pray the homosexuality away? The answer is no. Although your kid is attracted to the same gender, the premise behind the notion is that following a spiritual intervention, they're going to wake up and feel genuinely drawn to the opposing gender. Dr. Mills said in his years of expertise, this doesn't happen.

There are ways religion may play a part in your child's life. For example, some will opt to align their values and beliefs by sticking to their religion. As a consequence, they commit to living a heterosexual lifestyle. However, this doesn't affect their sexuality. Instead, it suggests they're loyal to their value system and beliefs. They don't pray the homosexuality away. Instead, they find a way to be homosexual and live a lifestyle compatible with their principles.

Learning your kid is LGBT may not mesh with your beliefs or belief system. However, it's likely exhibiting sympathy and affection. It's not often you'll regret delivering compassion, protection, and love. Likewise, you may love your kid without enjoying their habits.

Your kid is still your child. There hasn't been a metamorphosis in your youngster with this new knowledge. In truth, they may have been fighting with their ideas and feelings for years.

In other words, you've loved your homosexual kid, the difference is now you know they're gay. Who they are has not altered. This is still the kid you've cherished, loved, soothed, nourished, and been proud of and it may stay that way too.

Chapter 7.

Your response to the revelation that your kid is homosexual will likely have a huge influence on your child for years to come. Likewise, it may set the tone for your partnership eternally.

Be prepared by including these 5 strong ideas in your answer to your kid revealing, "I'm Gay

1. Communicate safety and unconditional love.

2. Approach the issue of being homosexual with interest. However, if you get it wrong, you may course-correct by providing a heartfelt apology. Remember, apologizing is not akin to approving their actions. Next, if you believe it is essential, acknowledge the fact that this is tough for you to talk about. Doing so promotes openness and may build an atmosphere of safety and trust.

3. Avoid probing inquiries, and be conscious of your tone of speech. If you're feeling too many emotions to think clearly, it's alright to go away from the discussion for a few minutes and return once you organize your ideas.

4. Remember, this is your kid, the same child they were just seconds before they informed you they're homosexual. Ideas like praying the homosexuality away are typically unpleasant and, in fact, fruitless.

5. Keep in mind that guilt and rejection do not alter sexual orientation. Instead, it generates alienation and pain that might deepen as time goes on. On the contrary, loving your kid without enjoying their actions or choices is always an option.

Chapter 8.

Modern dos and don'ts for parents of gay kids coming out

More LGBT individuals are coming out and coming out sooner than ever before in our nation. According to Statistics Canada, the number of same-sex families stepping up to be counted soared up 42.4 percent between 2006 and 2011. These more open examples of mainstream homosexual adulthood are providing young gay men and women the confidence to be honest and upfront about their sexuality, and are influencing the perceptions of the people they are coming out to. However, even for contemporary, progressive parents, some missteps may inflict unwarranted and sometimes inadvertent suffering. Coming out is a key stage that may frequently make or break the child-parent relationship. But don't worry parents! I've got a large homosexual handbook to assist you. I met together with two new generation homosexuals (Marie and Scott) in Canada's top secret gay headquarters (Starbucks) to get their view on current dos and don'ts for parents with queer kids coming out. These are their top five tips.

DO: Foster a positive LGBTQ environment

Homosexuality comes in different kinds and sizes. Stereotypical habits, attire, and hobbies aren't necessarily a consistent sign your youngster is a friend of Dorothy. tiny Jimmy may be swishy and end up straight, and just because tiny Molly likes softball doesn't imply she loves other girls. Instead, depend on your instincts as a parent. If you suspect your kid may be homosexual, one of the most essential things you can do is establish a gay-friendly atmosphere, you simply don't have to be blatant.

As Marie so eloquently says: "Create an atmosphere of diversity/openness in your house so your kids may feel safe if they are questioning. Instead of presuming someone has a boyfriend or girlfriend, use more gender-neutral language like 'So is there anybody at the party that you like?' or 'Is your buddy so-and-so dating someone new?' Don't assume everyone in the world is straight, and your kids will feel less out of place in your family."

It may be as simple as responding pleasantly or showing affinity with LGBT persons in the news or on TV. Scott says: "Casually emphasize your support of LGBTQ persons in general should it come up spontaneously.

Don't say anything negative that might make your son/daughter hesitate/reconsider coming out."

It's crucial to realize you can't push someone out of the closet. Coming out and getting out are two very different things. Be patient and let your homosexual souffle finish cooking before you open the oven door.

Don't: Say "I still love you no matter what"

This sounds like a lovely thing to say and it's something you will see a lot of in dramatizations on TV. But as Scott points out there is a subtext: "Saying 'I love you no matter what' says that your kid's gayness is something to be neglected in the name of love. It translates to 'I love you even if you are homosexual' as if gayness were a disease or anomaly." As for a proposed alternative? "How about simply 'Thank you for informing me. I adore you.'"

Don't: Make it about you

Coming out is a major moment in a homosexual person's life. For others, it ends up being the most crucial time in their life. It's a significant issue for parents too. Often moms and dads need time to adapt, be re-educated, and lament the loss of expectation they had for their baby.

But whatever you are going through, your son or daughter is undoubtedly going through something more intense and vital. Scott offers a perfect example telling me his parents were: "...embarrassed I didn't feel comfortable telling them sooner," adding, "They don't trust me as much because they're skeptical that I was hiding a big part of myself before coming out."

This is a perfect example of making it about oneself. Scott's parents are undoubtedly feeling horrible that they didn't cultivate a gay-positive atmosphere and are feeling a bit guilty about their son suffering in silence. While their attitude is considerably better than sending your child off to reparative treatment it still puts the spotlight on them and their troubles. Your difficulties as a parent certainly require attention, but putting it for a time helps while you and your kids adapt to a new dynamic.

DO: Open a discourse

This one is crucial. Getting comfortable with your kid's sexual identity needs discourse but there are some crucial things to follow.

It's vital to realize that sexuality may be a very private affair. Imagine discussing in the context of who you would prefer to have sex with with your parents. AWKWARD. If your kid or daughter doesn't feel comfortable talking to you right away, or if you don't feel comfortable talking about it right away, consider contacting another LGBT person or group (ex PFLAG).

This is a circumstance Marie encountered telling me, "Because I was away at school after coming out to my mom, I didn't have the experience of 'living with it' every day therefore I wasn't aware that she was truly dealing with it. But about a year ago she revealed to me that she did struggle with comprehending it at first, but that improved as she talked to other gay people and searched out resources for parents of LGBT people. They helped her realize that being homosexual doesn't impact who your son/daughter is."

Don't: Ask whether it is a phase

Your LGBT kid or daughter knows who they are attracted to the same way you do. Yes, sexuality exists on a continuum and yes it may be fluid, but if they are coming to you with this knowledge, it's fair to assume they are presently pretty sure.

Trying to modify your child's sexuality is one of the most destructive things you can do. There is a reason conversion treatment has startling rates of failure and a reason the federal government is seeking to outlaw it. It's also crucial not to seek a cause.

Marie says: "Don't presume or inquire whether your kids' sexuality was "caused" by anything. ie: asking if there was a terrible incident or relationship that led your child to "turn," (I believe this is extremely prevalent for homosexual women to be questioned) or if they simply "haven't met the right guy/girl yet."

These guidelines are aimed to smooth over some frequent speed bumps in the contemporary coming out process, however, not all Canadian kids are fortunate enough to have a family open to having a gay child or open to altering their beliefs about homosexuality.

Luckily our nation is filled with services to support LGBT youngsters through a challenging period that may often leave them homeless or suicidal. If you are a homosexual person in distress organizations like PFLAG Canada, Kids Help Phone, and Egale Canada are only a phone or click away.

Don't: Make it about you

One of the most typical responses from parents might be walking into a closet of their own, feeling the need to conceal the fact that their kid has just come out. Asking your kid not to tell other relatives or family friends about their sexuality, or to suppress the knowledge yourself, translates to one unambiguous and hurtful sentiment: I am embarrassed of you. What you can ask and should ask is whether it's OK for you to share this news with others.

While showing acceptance is vital, it's also imperative that the person coming out decides who knows and when for a process that can be extremely individualized and often stressful.